WILLIAM F. DUNNE and MORRIS CHILDS

Permanent Counter-Revolution

The Role of the Trotzkyites in the Minneapolis Strikes

CONTENTS

Foreword

The two militant strikes of truck drivers and helpers in Minneapolis – in May and July – have raised in the most pressing form the question of the relations between the Farmer-Labor state government, headed by Governor Floyd Bjornsterne Olson, and the labor movement.

The question arose in a particularly sharp form in the second strike – although it was present in the first strike and of basic strategic importance at that time. It came up because the Minneapolis Trades and Labor Assembly was and is dominated by Olson supporters who hold official positions in the trade union movement.

Both strikes involved several thousand newly organized workers and their wives and families. Both strikes had great popular support. In both strikes the workers conducted themselves with the greater resoluteness, heroism, and discipline. Up to the time Governor Olson sent in his troops and declared martial law, the strikers defeated the employers. They succeeded in the mass picketing, which was aided by great numbers of other workers and unemployed mobilized through the Unemployment Councils and the Communist Party, and in the physical combats with the police and other armed forces of the employers. Truck transportation moved only with the permission of the strike committee.

It is an axiom of working class struggle the better the organization of the workers' forces and the higher their morale, the greater is the guilt of the leadership for not obtaining the maximum results in the given circumstances, or for an actual defeat.

The Trotzkyite leadership of Truck Drivers and Helpers Union 574 cannot swear themselves loose from this guilt. Neither can they excuse their defeatist strategy and tactics by pleas of ignorance. Nor can they say that they were not warned of the consequences to the truck drivers and the labor movement as a whole of their toleration (to put it mildly) of Governor Olson and his official instruments in the Trades and Labor Assembly.

In estimating the extent of the Trotzkyite trifling with and ignoring of the most fundamental question of the labor and revolutionary movement – that of the class character of the government in any given epoch – we must keep in mind that this gentry pose as revolutionists. They pretend to be far more "revolutionary" than the Communist Party. They take the lead in slandering and vilifying Communists and the Communist International among more advanced workers. Furthermore, before the Minneapolis strike, they claimed they had discovered the magic method by which .revolutionists could work in the American Federation of Labor unions without coming info decisive clashes with "conservative" officialdom.

They sneered at the Communists who declared that the exposure of and struggle against the bureaucracy were necessary if the rank and file in any struggle was not to be confused, discouraged and betrayed.

The Trotzkyites laughed off all proposals to make clear the true anti-working class role of Governor Olson in the first strike. Even when he had the National Guard under arms these leaders kept their mouths shut.

From the very beginning, it was most necessary to prepare the workers for Olson's later military attack. This attack was sure to come if the truck drivers and their working class supporters pressed forward their demands and mass struggle for union recognition, higher wages, and better working conditions. Yet these Trotzkyites, although they claim to be revolutionists, did not remind the workers of what Marx and Engels wrote of the role of government: "The State – that is the executive committee of the ruling class."

In the first strike, in May, the Trotzkyite leaders, working closely with Olson's henchmen in the Trades and Labor Assembly, discouraged a general strike for which large numbers of workers and their unions were ready and had in fact already voted.

They signed a "truce" with the employers while Olson kept his troops mobilized. The truce turned out to be the end of the strike. It was hailed as a "victory" by the Trotzkyite press and by the official labor press.

The Trotzkyites wrote long articles in their press denouncing Communist critics of their conduct of the strike. They edged their way into "liberal" publications with glowing encomiums for themselves and sly slanders of the "Stalinites", of the "official Communists".

But the victory was a hollow one, as the Communists pointed out. The employers, and Olson, having carefully observed the tactics of the Trotzkyites, and having made their own estimate of the caliber of these leaders, arrived at the conclusion that it was not necessary even to comply with the *formal* terms of the "settlement". They refused to increase wages, they discriminated against union members, they refused to abide by working rules or classifications of employees.

They wanted another strike – a showdown. The union was forced to strike; but the probability of victory lay with the truck drivers. The

2

arbitrary attitude of the Citizens' Alliance and the employers generally had placed large sections of the population on the side of the workers, and the working class as a whole was ready to support their struggle.

From the outset, knowing that Olson and his troops would, if necessary, be used to decapitate the strike, the employers, the Minneapolis chief of police, and the Citizens' Alliance deliberately provoked the workers. Early in the strike, acting under orders to shoot to kill given them by Chief of Police Johannes, police shot into unarmed pickets, killing two and-wounding fifty or more.

Olson promptly brought in the troops. He declared martial law and authorized the issuing of permits for the moving of trucks. Something like 4,000 permits were issued – breaking the strike. A sham battle went on between Olson and the Citizens Alliance but the main objective had been reached – the-conduct of the strike was taken out of the hands of the unions.

Governor Olson's troops raided the headquarters of Local Union 574 and arrested something like two hundred leaders and active members. These were placed in a military stockade, and brought before military courts.

It was not until martial law was declared that the Trotzkyite leaders began to criticize: Olson. Even then their criticisms were mild, tempered and eclectic.

Their daily official strike publication was edited by one, Solow, until recently one of the editors of the *Menorah Journal* and a still more recent Trotzkyite acquisition. It had the crust to declare in a first page editorial – *after* martial law had been declared – that "the sole responsibility for martial law in Minneapolis rests on the shoulders of the *employers*". (Our emphasis.) *No responsibility on Olson, the governor who sent in the troops and who is their commander-in-chief!*

Even *after* martial law was in force, Goldman, the Trotzkyite lawyer from Chicago, was declaring at Minneapolis mass meetings that Olson was a product of contending class forces, that he had hesitated, that he had gone to the Right and to the Left, etc., "but that as long as he goes to the Left we will support him", et cetera, ad nauseum!

Why did the Trotzkyites lay off Olson? Ignorance? They know better. They laid off Olson because they were afraid to break with his henchmen in the Trades and Labor Assembly and appeal to the rank and file over their heads – as the longshoremen's leaders did in San Francisco and other West Coast ports. They thought they could treat with these people. They did, and they treated away the truck drivers' strike and the general strike that was necessary to drive out the troops and win the strike.

Only when it was too late, when the working class forces were confused and partially demoralized, did the Trotzkyite leaders raise the question of "a 48-hour sympathy strike".

On the other hand, the Communist Party position on the role of Governor Olson and the middle class Farmer-Labor administration that serves the interests of capitalism in its fight against the working class has been shown by life itself to be correct.

But one instance is needed to prove this contention:

Only in Minneapolis has a labor officialdom dared to take the position *openly* that the sending in of troops, the declaration of martial law, the raiding of union headquarters, mass arrests by the military, and the issuance of military permits to employers, had for their purpose the winning of the strike for the union!

This is what is actually peddled by the Minneapolis labor officialdom. The spread of this poisonous interpretation of military strike-breaking was made possible only by the Trotzkyite collaboration with Governor Olson's tools in the trade union movement.

At the present time, the A. F. of L. Executive Council, acting undoubtedly with the consent of Tobin, head of the International Union to which Local 574 belongs, has given a charter to gas station attendants (petroleum workers) who were organized into Local 574. The splitting process has begun. The Trades and Labor Assembly officialdom announces openly that if the A. F. of L. Executive Council and Tobin demand the dividing up of Local 574 into a half-dozen .unions they will line up for such a scheme. The Trotzkyites are now faced with the problem of fighting the officialdom or of surrendering organizationally – as they have politically.

Among the rank and file of the truck drivers and other Minneapolis workers there is the greatest disillusionment and hatred of Olson; but this does not as yet mean that they are ready to fight it out with his henchmen. They will not be ready to make this fight – and without such a fight they cannot really defeat the organized employers – until the Communists carry still further their campaign to make clear the elementary lessons of the two strikes, and mobilize the decisive sections of the working class around a genuine rank-and-file program of action.

This task calls for still clearer exposure of the anti-working class policy of the Trotzkyite leaders, and the refutation of the thousand lies and misrepresentations concerning the trade union policy and tactics of the Communist Party.

By raising with the utmost sharpness and clarity the whole question of the role of Governor Olson and the Farmer-Labor government in the May strike and the June strike, the Communist Party rendered a great service to the Minneapolis labor movement. The Party has begun to create the conditions for victory for the Minnesota working class in the great struggles which are right ahead of us.

Part 1

The Role of the Trotzkyites in the Minneapolis Strikes

I. Most Rapid Retreat of Leaders in U. S. History – From "General Strike" to Surrender in 24 Hours

The militant and splendidly organized strike of some 5,000 Minneapolis auto truck drivers and helpers, in May, 1934, which at one time showed strong signs of developing into a general strike of all trades, caused a crisis in the Minnesota state Farmer-Labor Party administration headed by Governor Olson, and threatened for a while to put a speedy end to his meteoric and demagogic career. The strike brought on a crisis in the ranks of the employers as a whole in Minneapolis, St. Paul and vicinity.

The Farmer-Labor Party administration and the employers escaped from the crisis at the expense of the working class by virtue of the policy of the Trotzkyites of the "Communist League" (the four Dunne brothers, with Cannon as their political adviser), whose leadership of Drivers Union 574 is a matter of record.

This policy, in spite of the efforts of the Communist Party, resulted in surrender to the employers, to Governor Olson, and to the official henchmen of Olson in control of the Central Labor Council; it resulted in the political and to some extent organizational isolation of the 5,000 drivers and their militant women's auxiliary, in the demobilization of the aroused working class – and in the loss of the major demands of the strikers.

The auto drivers struck for wage increases and recognition of their union. In the official settlement *no* wage increases are granted. But compulsory arbitration is instituted – as in the infamous automobile agreement engineered by Roosevelt and President Green of the American Federation of Labor. *The present wages are to stand for one year,* unless increases are "mutually agreed upon". Recognition is accorded –

to Clause 7A and the Minneapolis-St. Pal Regional Labor Board of the N.R.A.

This is a Trotzkyite victory! Will someone please page John L. Lewis of the United Mine Workers and President William Green and advise them of the advance of their policies in Minneapolis under the Trotzkyite banner?

Such a "victory" – and the thick crust which enables the Trotzkyites and their sheet to herald it as such – especially in view of the militancy of the strikers and the wide mass support accorded them – shows that these leaders are wallowing, and inviting workers to follow their example, in the same filthy pool of class cooperation as the official A. F. of L. leaders.

The shameful settlement had not the justification that the workers were *defeated*. Defeated workers have to make compromises that irk them. But the 5,000 drivers and their sympathizers, the large number of unemployed who fought side by side with them on the picket line, *had just begun to fight.*

They had inflicted a whole series of severe defeats upon the employers and their army of special deputies. The morale of the strikers was high. Relief was well organized. The building trades had declared a general strike.

There was mass sentiment for a general strike among the other unions affiliated to the Central Labor Council. More than half of those unions had voted for a general strike, according to reports.

To a considerable extent the strikers and their sympathizers controlled the streets. The class lines were tightly drawn. And, so bad are the economic conditions in Minneapolis, that even large sections of the lower middle class sympathized with the strikers – in whose ranks a large number of taxi drivers was already included.

So strong was popular sentiment in favor of the strikers, that the *Minneapolis Tribune* and the *Journal* – two of the most reactionary sheets in the country, running neck to neck with the *Chicago Tribune* for this honor – did not dare openly to attack the strike editorially during the whole duration of the struggle. When one C. A. Lyman, a well-known business man and clubman who had made the mistake of thinking that a special deputy's badge would prevent skull fracture while clubbing auto truck drivers on the picket line, was "killed in action", the *Tribune,* instead of the usual capitalist press demand for workers' necks in reprisal under such circumstances, dared only to publish a laudatory obituary.

The well-organized Minneapolis working class, which has a splendid tradition of struggle, had the opportunity of inflicting a severe defeat upon the employers, substantially improving their wages and working conditions, and strengthening the entire labor movement. The struggle would have spread to St. Paul where the workers are even better organized, and in the present period, when there is such ferment among all sections of the working class and big battles are the order of the day, the effect of such a powerful movement on the rest of the American working class is incalculable.

Near General Strike

The "truce" was agreed to, and the shameful settlement made before even the full strength of the auto truck drivers' union had been brought into play – to say nothing of the working class reserves.

One soldier sent in by Olson, one worker injured by troops, would have meant, in all probability, a general strike, victory for the labor movement, exposure and moral defeat of Olson and the Farmer-Labor Party administration. But this is what the Trotzkyite leaders were afraid of. If this is not so, why did they allow Governor Olson, during a truce – which in the military sense is supposed to stop all troop movements while it lasts – to mobilize the National Guard and keep it mobilized while the negotiations were going on?

Honest and capable leadership would have demanded the demobilization of the troops before one word was said about settlement of the strike. This was not done. Negotiations were carried on, the surrender was arranged with Governor Olson, while he held over the heads of workers the threat of military invasion.

The Trotzkyite leaders, thinking in terms of the Central Labor Council officials instead of in terms of the great mass of militant Minneapolis workers, quit cold like the palookas they are.

The working class reserves had not even gone into action when the fatal "truce" was agreed to. It spelled defeat.

The auto drivers and their working class supporters won on the field of action – in the street and on the picket lines. Their Trotzkyite leaders and Olson's henchmen in the Central Labor Council called off the battle and gave away the fruits of victory at conferences with Olson, the employers, and N.R.A. representatives.

Thanks to the policy of cowardice and capitulation of the American representatives of the still-born Trotzkyite "Fourth International", Governor Olson, one of the most dangerous enemies of the working class, and the whole Farmer-Labor Party bureaucracy, come out of this clash of class forces with flying colors, colors borne by the 3,700 National Guardsmen mobilized during the "truce" by this friend of the working class for use against the strikers.

The exposure and defeat of Olson should have been the central political objective of the Minneapolis struggle. This was the basic necessity for winning the economic demands for the Drivers' Union and the rest of the working class. Had Governor Olson dared to send a single soldier against the strikers and their supporters, the working class of Minneapolis would have answered with a general strike. He would have been driven from office. His upward climb on the backs of the workers and farmers would have been stopped for all time.

As it is, Olson is more firmly entrenched. The frightened employers have been given a breathing spell in which to reform their battle lines. The Central Labor Council demagogues were never put to the test of actually mobilizing strike action in support of the auto drivers. They heaved a sigh of relief and wiped the beads of cold sweat from their brows. Illusions in regard to N.R.A. have been strengthened.

Everything is lovely and the goose hangs high – everywhere except in the homes of the auto truck drivers and the unemployed workers who bore the cruel brunt of the struggle. Here is the decisive section of the shameful settlement:

> "In the hiring and discharging or laying off of employees, seniority rights shall prevail, *except for just cause....*
>
> "In the event that any employer affected hereby and its employees or their representatives cannot agree upon a wage scale or conditions of employment, such employer shall submit such subject or subjects to said *Minneapolis-St. Paul regional labor boar,^ for arbitration.* And also in the event that any dispute between said members of local union No. 5 74 and any employer affected hereby shall arise with reference to sections (1), (4) or (5) hereof, said parties hereto agree to submit such subject or subjects to *said board of arbitration. The board agrees to then immediately appoint two nominated employers, two nominated employees of local union No. 574, one labor board member and an industrial member of the board to such arbitration group, said arbitration group so constituted*

to name a seventh neutral member. Hearing on any arbitration hereinbefore referred to shall be called within five days after the appointment of said arbitration board. *When arbitration is completed, the board of arbitration shall report its decision to said regional labor board, which shall immediately make a final order in the premises in accordance with the said decision of said board of arbitration.*

"Hours of labor prevailing in the various business of the respective employers affected hereby shall be regulated by the respective codes applying thereto. *Any board of arbitration created by Section 6 hereof may inquire into all complaints for violation of said codes with respect to hours of employment, and shall file its report with proper federal authorities.*

"The term 'employees' as used herein shall include truck drivers and helpers, and such other persons as are ordinarily engaged in the trucking operations of the business of the individual employer. *Any dispute as to an interpretation of this section shall be referred to the regional labor board for determination.*

"The present-wage scale of each employer for the various classes of employees, until and unless changed by agreement between employers and employees, or the representatives of employees, or by arbitration as provided in Section 6 hereof, shall remain in force and effect for at least one year from date hereof."

How did this happen? What are the mechanics of a process which can turn victory for 5,000 workers – and potential victory for a huge section of the working class – into defeat overnight? How is it that with the employers on the defensive and the workers and their organizations masters of the situation one day, the strikers go to bed and wake up to find themselves defeated and bound with the galling chains of compulsory arbitration the next, with chains whose every link bears the tag, "Revolutionary Trade Unionism a la Trotzkyism"?

II. Minneapolis Example of Technique of Turning Offensive into Retreat, Victory to Defeat

The more one shuffles the cards dealt in the final showdown to the members of the Minneapolis Drivers and Helpers Union 574 in the militant struggle in which the whole working class had a stake, the clearer is the proof that the workers were cold-decked by James P. Cannon, his lieutenants in the leadership of the union, and Governor Olson and his Farmer-Labor Party henchmen in control of the Minneapolis Trades and Labor Assembly.

The panic-stricken retreat from a developing general strike situation to abject surrender to compulsory arbitration under the regional labor board *cannot be explained on the basis of a sudden shift in the relationship of class forces.*

It is the result of the inherent and incurable opportunism which is inseparable from the Trotzkyite position and which is its main ideological base. It is all the more menacing to workers who come under the influence of its priests and altar boys, as the Minneapolis defeat shows, since these artful rascals can even be yelling for a general strike while they prepare the machinery to make it impossible. This is the practical result for workers of opportunism covered by revolutionary phrases.

Truce Meant Defeat for Workers

The signing of the "truce", after the building trades council had declared a sympathetic strike and the general strike sentiment was mounting in the other unions, disrupted the working class ranks and spelled death for the main demands of the auto truck drivers and helpers. That the general strike was on the order of the day in Minneapolis is admitted by the Trotzkyite sheet for May 26. It says under a Minneapolis date line:

> "'The rank and file of the unions are ready for this action and it is possible that they may go out in a day or two."

To show by a number of facts the general upsurge that was taking place in the labor movement – and to one who knows the Twin Cities they are of the greatest significance – we quote again from this sheet:

> "The St. Paul drivers voted to go out but failed to do so at the last minute and agreed to arbitrate a point or two.... The street car men (Minneapolis) made a similar decision. The labor movement seethes with in-

dignation against the leaders responsible for these actions in the face of the situation created by the drivers' strike."

In regard to the possibility of a general strike, Cannon wired from Minneapolis on May 22 that "sentiment for it is spreading like wildfire". He stated further in the same dispatch: *"If the negotiations fail a general strike of sympathy with the drivers may result."*

We can show by their own statements that the shameful settlement and surrender of the strikers to N.R.A. and compulsory arbitration were not the result of a defeated strike. We can show that it bore no relation to the actual disposition of class forces at the time. An editorial in the "Communist" League sheet for May 26 says"

> "In pitched battles last Saturday and again on Monday the strikers fought back and held their own. And on Tuesday they took, the offensive, with devastating results.... 'Business men' volunteering to put the workers in their place and college boys out for a lark – as special deputies – to say nothing of the uniformed cops – handed over their badges and fled in terror before the mass fury of aroused workers.... A second feature of the fight at the City Market... is the fact that the whole union went into action on the picket line in mass formation; thousands of other union men went with them.... It is not a strike of the men alone but of the women also."

Does the foregoing – and the general facts are corroborated from all other sources – sound as if the 5,000 auto truck drivers were in a position which made it necessary for them to surrender?

On the contrary, it shows that the striking Drivers' Union and huge sections of the working class were *on the offensive. Leaders who surrender while their forces are on the offensive are either fools crooks or both. There were plenty of all three types in the Minneapolis struggle, as we shall see.*

The "truce" was signed under these conditions: the strike of the drivers – the militant core of the whole movement – was over, negotiations began, the working class forces were demobilized and the strikers' demands went splashing into the slimy pool of class collaboration.

The "truce" was signed only to be violated by Governor Olson. What kind of a truce is it when the enemy is allowed to bring up powerful reinforcements while the working class and its organizations are disarmed? Speaking of the National Guard, the *Minneapolis Journal* on May 26 said:

> *"Almost simultaneously with the mobilization order was a truce agreement* between the employers and strikers under which no trucks were moved and *mass picketing discontinued. This truce continued until a settlement was reached."* [My emphasis – B.D.]

We have seen what the settlement was – wages to remain as at present for one year and compulsory arbitration.

As soon as Governor Olson entered the situation, backed by two infantry regiments and one of artillery, the shameful retreat of the leaders began. Having signed the "truce" jointly with the officials of the Central Labor Council and thus made a united front with Olson's henchmen, the Trotskyite leaders committed themselves to the negotiations while some of their own striking followers were being called to the armories as members of the National Guard!

The calling of the troops put Governor Olson at the mercy of the organized labor movement. Under no circumstances could have defended this action by himself.

Trotzkyite Whitewash

It remained for the Trotzkyites and the Central Labor Council officials to furnish the formula with which the whitewash for Olson was mixed. This is what it was:

> "Governor Olson has got to make a showing, or Roosevelt will send in federal troops from Fort Snelling."

This typically opportunist formula was circulated widely among the strikers.

The next little job was to liquidate the general strike sentiment. Once more Cannon and the local Dunne dynasty furnished the required explanation. (We wish readers would scrutinize this counterrevolutionary contribution carefully because we shall encounter it again and again in the United States as the present struggles develop.) Here it is – mouthed over and over again by these leaders to get all its delicious flavor and then expectorated into the clean arena of the class struggle where so far the main slogan had been "general strike".

"We can't have a general strike because there is no revolutionary situation."

That general strikes produce revolutionary situations was not hinted. An extension of their slogan was formulated as:

"You can't fight bayonets with empty bellies."

The defeatist character of this combination of slogans and rumors circulated by the Trotzkyite leaders and the Central Labor Council officials is obvious. They were designed to halt the growing mass movement and they accomplished their purpose.

Even the propaganda for a general strike circulated by the renegade-dominated Drivers Union was definitely limited. We quote from their leaflet entitled "Conciliation, But *No* Surrender, Offered by Strikers to End Strike and Disorder":

> *"We call on every employed worker in Minneapolis not under contract to lay down his tools. To declare a holiday."* [My emphasis – B.D.]

For sheer anti-working class originality in devising ways and means of forming a united front with the treacherous bureaucrats of the labor movement this slogan is in a class by itself. Worship of the "sanctity of the labor contract" – the traditional shibboleth of the most treacherous official labor leaders in their efforts to keep workers' ranks divided – has never been carried out with such reverence even by Tobin himself, the head of the A. F. of L. union, to which Drivers Union 574 is affiliated.

There was a fourth slogan. Without the real defeatist character of the sentiment being explained to the strikers – and, of course, not to the rest of the organized workers – the lying statement was widely circulated that: "We have won 90 per cent of our demands."

By these propaganda methods the general strike situation was liquidated, Governor Olson's face was saved, the drivers' strike defeated, and compulsory arbitration fastened upon them. Arrested workers were fined and given workhouse sentences.

The capitalist press was jubilant. It had a right to be. *What it and the employers had believed to be a new revolutionary leadership in process of formation had proved to be of the same gutless and unprincipled character as that which they had been dealing with for years.*

III. Trotzky Group United with Olson Machine in A. F. of L to Send Back Minneapolis Strikers

The 'truce" having been signed jointly with the officials of the Central Labor Council by the Trotzkyite leaders of Drivers Union 574, the picket lines were called in while Governor Olson maintained three regiments of National Guardsmen under arms. The movement for a general strike was demobilized by methods already described.

The "truce" itself, in addition to being entirely one-sided in view of the military mobilization, simply called for no attempted movement of auto trucks by the employers – *trucks already stopped by the strike.*

The next step was to put over the "agreement". The methods by which this was accomplished would do credit to Edward McGrady, Assistant Secretary of Labor, and other highly skilled mechanics in the trade of making workers think they have won something long enough to vote against their own interests.

It is not too much to say that the militant truck drivers, who had cleaned the streets of professional scabs, special deputies, and astonished cops, and tied up truck transportation tighter than a bull's eye in fly time, were stunned by the sudden right-about-face of their leaders. The strikers, of course, did not know that the strategy of their leaders was to avoid conflict with the henchmen of Governor Olson in control of the Central Labor Council, to avoid open conflict with Olson at all costs; and to establish a broader base for their anti-working class activities in the labor movement, regardless of whether the immediate economic and political aims of the workers were sacrificed.

In other words, with all the appropriate but meaningless democratic gestures, *these leaders prevailed upon the strikers to accept while undefeated a settlement which runs counter to the interests of the drivers,* the whole labor movement, and the entire working class. They did this in order that the special and separate anti-working class political interests of the Trotzkyite group might have a working class base – 5,000 organized truck drivers – in which to find sanctuary and from which to conduct forays against the Communist Party and its leadership.

"Inside" Strategy

The pursuit of this objective of course fitted perfectly into the general crassly opportunistic policy followed throughout the strike in the relations with Governor Olson and his tools in the Central Labor Council. Not the least important aspect of this policy has to do with the question of "inside" strategy, that is, *the description of the Minneapolis tac-*

tics given to the membership of the Trotzkyite group by its official organ in New York City and in signed articles by Cannon, contrasted with what was *actually being done* on the field of action.

In a dispatch dated May 22, published in their sheet for May 26, Mr. Cannon is quoted as follows:

> "In a move to head off the general strike the regional labor board, on direct orders from Washington, is attempting to bring about a settlement. Dunne (V. R.), Skoglund and other militant leaders of the union have consistently explained the strike-breaking role of this agency and are warning the strikers now to watch out for any trap it may set for them."

In the same issue, under a Minneapolis date line of May 20, we find the following:

> "The swift developments of the strike are putting the governor on the spot. Whether or not to call out the militia – *he can't decide.* No reliance can be placed upon the governor or the labor board to settle anything favorably for the workers." [My emphasis – B.D.]

As we say, this appeared in the Trotzkyite sheet for May 26. *On that very day,* the Minneapolis *Journal* carried the following headline: *"Strike Settled, Thousands Back at Work; Trucks Moving Mountains of Goods."*

On this very day, while the Trotzkyite sheet was still trying to delude the workers, Governor Olson had shown that he could "decide". He had mobilized three regiments of troops – as Cannon and his lieutenants knew he would. Only they failed to prepare the workers for it and tell them that he would.

On this very day, May 26, the workers had been maneuvered into accepting the shameful settlement which did not contain, but which on the contrary ignored, more than "90 per cent of our demands".

The N.R.A. regional board had been recognized by the leaders of the strike and yet the drivers had been turned over to it and compulsory arbitration with their wage demands ignored. "The strike-breaking role of this agency" had been conveniently ignored.

Governor Olson was whitewashed at the time his troops were under arms. The issues which would have produced general strike action over the heads of the Central Labor Council and State Federation of

Labor officials, which would have exposed and defeated Olson and brought victory, were shoved deliberately into the background.

It Wasn't the Strikers Who Quit

It is very interesting and informative, in this connection, to read the account in the Minneapolis *Journal* – a paper which cannot be accused of bias toward the strikers – of the reception by the union membership of the settlement terms and the method by which they were put across. We quote:

"The union's strike committee, which had been in session throughout Friday, announced an acceptance of the peace terms shortly after 6 p.m. What took place in the strike committee meeting we do not know, but the 24-hour session shows that *there must have been much opposition to the proposed settlement in this committee.*"

We quote further from the *Journal:*

"Shortly after a vote by acclamation was taken of the crowd at the strike headquarters. *It was so close that William Brown, president of the union, did not want to be governed by it.*"

According to Sender Garlin of the *Daily Worker* staff, who was present at this time, there was nothing close about it – it was definitely *against* the agreement.

"During- the mass meeting discussion preliminary to the vote on the agreement," continues the *Journal, "the opposition became so vociferous that there was doubt the agreement would be ratified."*

The opposition came from the rank and file who were *still thinking in terms of the general strike.* Did the Trotskyite leaders of the union, in their stage role of "principled Communists", expose the rotten terms of the settlement?

Don't ask foolish questions, comrades! Listen to the joyous announcement of the proceedings in the *Journal:*

"*The strike leaders favored acceptance* and urged the men to realize that it offered the union some important concessions. [A study of the agreement fails to disclose these "concessions," – B.D.] The plea was

16

made that the agreement is *'an important first step* [in what direction was not stated – B.D.] and it was pointed out that *rejection meant a long and perhaps uncertain battle. It was the plea of the strike leaders that finally brought ratification by the big crowd."*

The phrase "an important first step" is part of the counterfeit coin with which the leaders short-changed the strikers.

This is final and clinching proof that Cannon and his local lieutenants are responsible for the defeat and surrender before the struggle had even begun to reach its peak. Cannon was in Minneapolis at the time. He was in a caucus with V. R. Dunne and others while the meeting was in progress. G. J. Dunne was left at the meeting to see that the shameful settlement went over as smoothly as possible.

What happened was simply this:

Governor Olson's Central Labor Council henchmen, loyal to their master and afraid of the growing mass movement, knew that Olson was through politically with the working class if he ever sent in troops. They knew that if he had to choose in the case of a general strike, or even the continuation of the strike of auto driver and building tradesmen, Olson *would* send in troops for the propertied class; in other words, that he would find his class level. They therefore flatly told Cannon and his lieutenants that they would oppose by all means any extension of the struggle.

As the Zulus say, "their bellies turned to water". Thinking mainly in terms of this *more conservative leadership"* (as Cannon's sheet describes these hard-boiled bureaucrats), the Trotzkyite leader-folded up. They forgot all their brave words and pledged themselves to "go along" with this "more conservative leadership".

They wrote another miserable page in the history of class collaboration in the labor movement. After all, picket lines alone cannot substitute for revolutionary politics. With one gesture the Trotzkyite leaders nullified the days and nights of heroic struggle by thousands of workers.

Cannon, self-appointed representative of the "Fourth International", deserter from the ranks of revolutionary fighters, maligner of the Communist Party of the U.S.A. and the Communist International, was mainly responsible for this shameful fiasco. He can have his "settlement". Let him try to justify it to the members of Drivers' Union 574 and the rest of the Minneapolis working class three months from the day it was slipped over on them!

As for the four Dunne brothers, speaking only of the question of competency as leaders, the four Marx brothers would have done a better job for the strikers. Harpo at least knows enough to keep his mouth shut. None of these comedians has as yet been caught putting into the mouths of workers the stool-pigeon statement that "these 'Communists' are in the pay of the bosses", as the Trotzkyite sheet does in its issue for May 26.

IV. Trotzkyite Sheet Conceals Part Played by Olson, Farmer-Labor Governor, in Defeating the Great Minneapolis Strike Movement

If Ignatius Loyola, founder of the Society of Jesus, were alive today, even his cassock would turn green with envy after reading the latest number of the Trotzkyite sheet. In that issue, issued *after* the Minneapolis surrender, by the negative process so dear to the Jesuit heart, Cannon and his lieutenants, by not even so much as mentioning Governor Olson and the historical fact that he mobilized three regiments of National Guardsmen against the strikers, grant amnesty to this potential mass murderer. By this device they give support to him, the Farmer-Labor Party government in Minnesota, and to its henchmen in official positions in the labor movement.

As a matter of fact, the National Guard was kept mobilized in Minnesota – under the pretense of enforcing an embargo on the shipment of cattle into the State from other drought-stricken regions.

If Cannon and the Dunne brothers were the ordinary type of trade union bureaucrats, we would not put so much emphasis on this point. But they call themselves the "Communist" League and claim to have charted the only road by which the American working class can march to power. They claim that we "Stalinists" of the Communist Party have forgotten and perverted the revolutionary teachings of Lenin. They claim that they are the only bearers of "true" Leninism.

We have dealt to same extent with the capitulation to the employers' association and Governor Olson, engineered by the Trotzkyite leaders in the Drivers' Union 574, Cannon, and the officials of the Central Labor Council; the surrender of the strikers to compulsory arbitration and the regional labor board; the systematic and deliberate sabotage of the general strike, and the demobilization of the mass movement long before it reached its peak.

Taken in connection with the present wide mass movement of struggle of American workers against intolerable living conditions and for elementary political rights, this was one of the most serious recent setbacks suffered by the working class. It was a needless retreat engineered by spineless and unprincipled leaders. The thought of surrender did not originate among the fighting masses of workers in the ranks of the unions and the Unemployment Councils.

Questions of Vital Importance

Involved in this action are tactical questions of the highest importance – questions having to do with the speed, the methods and the direction of the vast strike movement in this country. Yet, for the revolutionary movement, the issues raised *by omission* in the Trotzkyite sheet for June 2 are of still greater importance.

Is Olson the executive head of capitalism's State machinery in Minnesota or isn't he?

Did Governor Olson mobilize three regiments (at least) of troops for use against the strikers and were not the "settlement" negotiations conducted under the threat of military force? Or is this a falsehood?

Is it not a fact that henchmen of Olson and the Farmer-Labor Party in official positions in the Central Labor Council and elsewhere were determined to stop the general strike so as not "to put Olson up against it"?

Is it not a fact that rather than appeal to the rank and file over the heads of these leaders, the Trotzkyites agreed to the "truce" and advised workers to accept the official terms of surrender?

In the Trotzkyite sheet for June 2, is there a single word or phrase that says or hints, directly or indirectly, anything about these decisive facts of the Minneapolis struggle? *There is not!*

This is nothing more nor less than a deliberate attempt to conceal from workers the identity of the main enemy. It leaves the enemy undisturbed in his prepared positions, from which, *camouflaged* as a friendly force during the period of "peace", he can advance once more upon workers in the next struggle.

One more question:

Where, in the writings or speeches of Lenin, is there to be found anything that can be interpreted as endorsement of a policy of concealing from workers – before, during or after a battle – the identity of the main enemy, the direction of his position, his strategy and tactics?

Nowhere! For the simple reason that this is a counter-revolutionary, and, therefore, anti-working class policy. The apostles of the "Fourth" International use "realistic" trade union tactics that result in hailing as a victory the forced acceptance of compulsory arbitration by a union through official maneuvers and under threat of military invasion. But they do not like the word "counterrevolutionary" when applied to them, to their policy and their tactics in the American class struggle. They will work up a most fervent moral indignation against the use of the term in connection with the Minneapolis struggle.

But why should we mince words when dealing with a case in which the facts are so clear as to admit of no argument? In our simple-minded way, we cannot see any great difference between A. F. of L. officials' silent whitewashing of the governors who called out troops against workers and ruined farmers in New Mexico, Iowa, Wisconsin, Pennsylvania, etc., and the Trotzkyite amnesty granted Governor Olson – with this exception:

Governor Olson is the titular head of a party which *pretends* to oppose the two big capitalist parties and protect the interest of workers and poor farmers. It is all the more necessary to expose his real role. This is elementary.

The Trotzkyite amnesty also includes the Farmer-Labor bureaucrats in the Minneapolis unions. As in the case of Olson, there is not even a hint that they did not support the drivers' strike one hundred per cent. The whole question of the Minneapolis general strike, of the troop mobilization, of the relationship of class forces, is dropped like a hot potato by the Trotzkyite sheet for June 8 – *published one meek after the end of the strike.*

But in *Toledo* – that is another question! About the situation in *Toledo* there are more brave words. The Trotzkyites are in favor of a general strike – in *Toledo!* Governor White is flayed as an enemy who threatens to use force against the workers. In *Toledo,* says the Trotzkyite sheet, "the strikebreaking role of the labor board [with whose Minneapolis counterpart they induced workers to sign a compulsory arbitration agreement, without a wage increase] and its multi-millionaire agent Charles P. Taft... must be exposed."

In *Toledo,* says the Trotzkyite sheet, "the A. F. of L. bureaucracy must not be permitted to postpone the general strike any longer. Nothing can be expected from the strike-breaking labor board..." No compromise in *Toledo.*

Well, well, well! The smell is not any more pleasant but the visibility is better. It is now clear that strikebreaking governors, strike-breaking labor boards and strike-breaking A. F. of L. bureaucrats are encountered only by workers in those localities where such demons have not been exorcised by the bell, book and candle of the Trotzkyite ritual. Let a few archangels of the Fourth (Dimensional) International appear on the scene and bayonets behind a Farmer-Labor Party governor become a boon so sacred that it cannot even be mentioned in mundane print.

This is the same process, on a smaller scale, which, accompanied by slanderous attacks on the Communist Party and the Communist International, cleared the road down which German fascism marched over the bodies of tortured and murdered workers. The Farmer-Labor governor and his troops are a "lesser evil" than the wicked employers and their special deputies,

More Than a "Tendency"

There is something more here than a tendency. The omission of all criticism of Governor Olson – even the mention of the bare facts – and of the Farmer-Labor bureaucracy in the Trotzkyite sheet at a time when the strike settlement makes workers anxious to know the role played by every person prominent in the struggle, constitutes an alliance with Olson and his machine. Whether it is temporary or permanent does not matter so far as the principle is concerned.

Can Trotzkyites plead ignorance of the anti-working class character of the Olson program – the Olson whose immediate ambition is to lead a national Farmer-Labor Party movement? It is ridiculous. They know that he is a conscienceless demagogue. They know of the underworld and capitalist connections of his machine.

They know that Olson will tolerate almost any kind of criticism from Communists – if they refrain from calling him an enemy of the working class. They know that Olson has tried again and again to maneuver with the Communist Party with the object of fooling workers into believing that it considers him a "friend of labor."

They know that in 1923-24 Olson himself and his principal henchmen in the Minneapolis labor movement time and time again solicited an endorsement from Comrade Ruthenburg, leader of the Communist Party, from this writer, from C. A. Hathaway and others. So insistent were he and his supporters at one time, that the Party District Bureau met, made a decision in regard to him and his program and conveyed its *adverse verdict* to him formally by a committee in order to put a stop to the rumors spread by his supporters. These decisions of the District Bureau were made public.

At that time Olson had never been forced to show his true colors in a decisive situation involving the lives and liberties of workers on strike. But the Party gauged him and his movement correctly. Today he looks around again for some kind of revolutionary camouflage. The Minnesota air is charged with hectic phrases about "monopoly", "the evils of capitalism", "the beast of Wall Street", the "rise of the class struggle", etc. These phrases roll easily from the lips of venal leaders who received their early training in a State where the Socialist Party organization supported the Left Wing, where the State secretary and others went to prison for opposing conscription, where there was mass opposition to the Morgan-Wilson war.

The farmers are bankrupt and demand action. The recent drivers' strike, the sympathetic strike of the building trades and other workers, the wide mass sentiment for a general strike, brought on a crisis in class relationships.

Governor Olson is looking for a "Communist" label to add to his collection. The Trotzkyites, at least for the last week, allowed him to wear their forged label pinned to the same coat from which dangles the badge of Commander-in-Chief of the Minnesota National Guard.

This is treachery and the working class will deal with it in the way the working class always does when it frees itself from the influence of its enemies.

V. The Party Leadership Analyzed

The tremendous support, moral and material, received by the strikers of Drivers' Union 574 from practically all sections of the Minneapolis working class – support whose volume was still growing at the time the shameful settlement was negotiated, and put over on the strikers by the Trotzkyite and Central Labor Council leaders – the rapid development and indomitable spirit of the main section of the strike, show that in Minneapolis *there had arrived one of those moments when the working class is ready for deeds that make high points in the history of the class struggle.*

The Party District has organized and led some splendid mass struggles – hunger marches to the State capital, relief struggles, etc. It had an important role in the struggles of the St. Paul packinghouse workers. It has exposed the anti-working class character of Olson's Farmer-Labor Party government before large numbers of workers. The Communist Party members have access to many A. F. of L. unions, and workers listen eagerly to Communist Party speakers.

But the Communist Party leadership in the Minneapolis District did not gauge correctly the militant temper of the working class and did not foresee clearly the outbreak of the struggle, and therefore could not fully prepare the working class for it.

Party Responsibility

In this sense the Communist Party, although its members fought heroically side by side with the strikers on the picket line, although the Communists in the International Labor Defense rendered great services in the struggle, and the Communist Party fraction in the Unemployment Councils mobilized the unemployed in support of the strike, the Party District was unable to expose clearly the disastrous influence of the Cannon-Dunne leadership. *It was only by consistent work within the union of the drivers and in the other unions that their defeatist policy could have been efficiently exposed and thwarted.* As it was, the agitation, propaganda and work of the Party District, in the main correct, came for the most part from outside the main body of striking workers.

The Party District was not keenly aware of the developing wide mass support for the strike of Drivers Union 574. The pent-up resentment of the working class was released. The sympathetic strike declared by the building trades council is evidence of this. It had failed to estimate correctly the growing will of the workers to battle for the right to organize and for better wages and working conditions. It seems to have failed to sense at the beginning of the struggle the great feeling of the masses for solidarity with the Drivers Union, who were, so to speak, the shock troops of the working class offensive.

The Party District issued a call for general strike. There can be no doubt that this general strike leaflet attempted to bring some political clarity into the struggle and placed the question of the general strike as the next and necessary form of struggle against the employers, the threat to the elementary rights of workers and their organizations, and Governor Olson's mobilization of the National Guard for use against the strikers.

Party Demands

The leaflet raised the following demands: Higher pay and improved working conditions; union recognition in all industries and shops in Minneapolis; stopping the police terror against workers; struggle against Governor Olson's threat to use the militia to break the strike;

no compulsory arbitration through the national or regional N.R.A. labor boards.

The leaflet called also for the election of rank-and-file committees – but did not tell workers why such committees were necessary. It did not give the names of the official leaders who were, one way or another, sabotaging the general strike movement. It did not point out that the general strike against the use of troops was the main weapon of the working class; *that it was necessary to assure victory for the drivers.* The leaflet did not point out the anti-working class character of the Farmer-Labor Party government and its hangers-on in the labor movement.

It was only after the drivers' strike had started that Communist Party members joined the union, and most of these were unemployed. There was no organized work of the Party comrades as a fraction and consequently no rank-and-file opposition group was formed.

Most important of all, because of lack of any substantial and active group of workers in the Drivers Union, it was difficult win support for the Party program in the militant core of the whole strike movement, in whose support the slogan of general strike found its most powerful appeal.

As a result of all this, the surrender of the Trotzkyite leaders and the Central Labor Council officials to Governor Olson, the regional labor board of the N.R.A. – and consequently to the employers – met only *unorganized* opposition.

There can be but one explanation of this. The Party District either did not know what was going on or if it did, it did not consider it important. It was not *politically* aware of the situation. He did this happen? We venture to suggest that the Open Letter can guide us to an understanding of what the situation was in respect to the splendid strike struggle of the drivers and to the relations to the other trade unions there. We quote:

> "Because in the Party, and particularly among the leading cadres, there is a *deep-going lack of political understanding* of the necessity of strengthening our basis among the decisive sections of the American workers. From this follows the fact that the leadership of the Party has not adhered to a fixed course for overcoming the main weaknesses of the Party, *allows itself to be driven by events,* and does not work out carefully with the comrades of the lower organizations

ways and means for the carrying through of resolutions and checking up on their execution."

It is clear that thousands of auto truck drivers, helpers, gas station workers, etc., were looking for leadership and a militant program as a way out of their unbearable conditions. Workers in such a situation will find leaders.

With the exception of militant workers, honestly trying to find the way out, but whose lack of experience in dealing with demagogues and the maneuvers of misleaders is always a great handicap, no one but Communists uncompromisingly fight for the immediate interests of the masses and for their general interests – the struggle for power – as well.

Unless the Communist Party members are able to influence decisively the course of such struggles as that in Minneapolis, no matter how great the heroism and determination of the workers, they are led invariably into a blind alley. If the millions of the working class could, by themselves, without leadership, find and use the correct methods for the advance against capitalism, there would be no need for Communist Parties and the Communist International. Failing to secure Communist leadership, but needing leaders, workers accept, especially in periods of intense class struggle, even corrupt, crooked, cowardly and ignorant leaders. This is bad for the working class. It helps to maintain the influence of the capitalist class, sometimes direct and brazen, sometimes, as in Minneapolis, watered down so it will not gag masses of workers already skeptical of the right of capitalism's mandate to rule forever.

This explains, partially at least, the comparative ease with which the Trotzkyites were able to organize and then mislead some thousands of militant workers. That they will retain this influence is unthinkable. But the weakness of the factory and trade union work of the Minneapolis Party District will have to be overcome speedily.

These Trotzkyites are really an unofficial wing of the Socialist Party and in this country a sort of extended arm of social-democracy in the labor movement. According to their official sheet, they went through a trying period of soul struggles trying to decide in which parade they would march on International May Day.

They marched on May First under the banner of the Socialist Party – behind the reformist banners held aloft by James Oneal, Norman Thomas, Algernon Lee, Judge Panken, the New Leader and the Daily Forward.

The Trotzkyite call for a fourth international is nothing more or less than a covering for the discredited elements of the Second International. *It is an attempt to create what in military parlance is called a "diversion"* – an attempt to distract the attention of the working class from the main issues of the class struggle and check the march of the more advanced workers to Communism. Their support and brotherly coaching of the chauvinist American Workers Party is but a recognition of kinship in a variant clique that has the same purpose, blocking the revolutionary path of the masses.

The All-Important Question of Organization

Perhaps no recent struggle has shown with such peculiar appropriateness the need for the daily application of the only method of carrying out a correct Party line, emphasized by Comrade Stall at the Seventeenth Congress of the Communist Party of the Soviet Union, as has the relation of the Minneapolis Party District to the recent mass struggles:

> "After the correct line has been given, after a correct solution of the problem has been found, success depends on the manner in which the work is organized, on the organization of the struggle for the application of the line of the Party, on the proper selection of workers, on supervising the fulfillment of decisions of the leading organs. Without this the correct line of the Party and the correct solutions are in danger of being severely damaged. More than that, after the correct political line has been given, the organizational work decides everything, including the fate of the political line itself, *i.e.,* its success or failure."

VI. Background and Perspective of Minnesota Labor

The strategic importance of Minnesota in the mass struggles of workers and ruined farmers today makes the defeatist policy and acts of the Trotzkyites and the Central Labor Council officials in the recent strikes all the more damaging. The Twin Cities – St. Paul and Minneapolis—have a population of about a million. The working class population is a big majority. The hundred-mile circle which includes the Twin Cities is a densely populated area whose workers and toiling agriculturists are dominated by the elevator and milling combines, the power monopoly and the railroads.

In the northern part of the State the Oliver Iron Mining Co., a subsidiary of United States Steel, reigns supreme. Duluth is the head of Great Lakes transportation for iron ore and wheat.

Before Minnesota was admitted to Statehood the rape of its magnificent white pine forests by the lumber barons (completed later by the Weyerhauser combine) had already begun. They robbed even the Indian reservations of their timber, they bought State legislatures, governors, congressmen and senators. They paid lumber workers a pittance and piled up huge fortunes for themselves. They cut and slashed without regard for anything but immediate profit. For years they took only the clear butt logs and left trunk sections and limbs to furnish fuel for a series of forest fires which destroyed whole towns. Today white pine is so scarce and valuable that the Mississippi is dredged for "dead-heads" – logs waterlogged and sunk during the drives to the mills. The rape by the lumber barons was followed by the robbery of public lands carried out by the Great Northern and Northern Pacific railways.

Iron ore was discovered in huge quantities in the cut-over timber area and what the railways had overlooked the steel trust stole. Flour mills replaced lumber mills. Pulp and paper plants sprang up utilizing the second growth timber for its raw material, electric light and power interests found water-power galore and a wide field for their product. Minnesota was industrialized. The Twin Cities are the third largest railway center in this country.

Minnesota politics for years were dominated by the inner conflicts between these various exploiting interests – conflicts carried on inside the Republican and, to a lesser extent, the Democratic parties. About 1912 the Socialist Party developed great influence in Minneapolis and St. Paul – a reflection of the rapid development of a working class and its struggle against trust capital. Its influence in the St. Paul labor movement – especially among railwaymen – was powerful. In Minneapolis labor the S.P. was the dominant force.

In the struggle inside the Socialist Party during the War the Minnesota State organizations supported the Left Wing. So strong was the opposition to the war and to Gompers' efforts to tie the labor movement to the war machine, that Gompers was compelled to make a special trip to the Twin Cities to combat it. It was in the struggle over the formation of the "American Alliance for Labor and Democracy", the special instrument for winning the unions in support of the Morgan-Wilson war program, that the present lineup in the officialdom of the Minneapolis labor movement began to take shape. Masses of workers and farmers were opposed to the war. The political reflection of this was seen in the antiwar book written by Congressman Lindbergh (father of the flying son-in-law of a House of Morgan partner), in the pacifist activities of the Nonpartisan League – the farmers' organization formed by ex-socialists, etc. Clever careerists like Van Lear, a former socialist mayor of Minneapolis, I. G. Scott, Bastis, etc. – prominent union men, aldermen and former socialists – formed an alliance with the Nonpartisan League, launched the Minneapolis *Daily Star* and began the maneuvers which resulted in the formation of the Farmer-Labor Party.

The Communist Party then favored the formation of a farmer-labor party. But it quickly became clear that this would inevitably be a party protecting the interests of big capital and would lead the working class away from the revolutionary path, deeper into the morass of reformist parliamentarism. The C.P. withdrew all support from the movement.

But even in this period elementary democracy prevailed in the trade union movement of the Twin Cities. There were strong Communist fractions in the Central Labor Unions of St. Paul and Minneapolis. Communist Party speakers had practically unrestricted access to these organizations and their affiliated unions. The Left Wing in the A. F. of L. unions was powerful.

In 1920-21 the Minneapolis Trades and Labor Assembly organized and financed a speaking and organizational tour for the writer throughout Minnesota in behalf of the Mooney Defense Committee, raising the issue of a general strike for his release.

Following the federal raid on and arrests of delegates to the Communist Party convention in Bridgeman, Mich., in 1922, the Minneapolis Central Labor Council wired the writer in jail that they had raised $1,000 towards bail of $10,000. Finances for bail and defense of C. E. Ruthenberg, William Z. Foster, and other indicted Communists were raised by Minneapolis unions. Many prominent trade unionists, including the editor of the official paper, professed support of and even at times defended the Communist Party.

In the nationwide strike of railway shopmen in 1922, nowhere was there more militancy, or greater mass support than in Minneapolis and St. Paul.

But as the Farmer-Labor organization acquired more vested interests, as the possibility of official careers took on concrete form, as more and more trade union leaders were elected or appointed to office (Mahoney, mayor of St. Paul, the inclusion of practically all the Minneapolis labor officialdom in the Farmer-Labor Party bureaucracy, etc.), a fight against the Communist Party was begun.

The campaign to rid the unions of all revolutionary workers, and thereby behead the struggle against the policy of "worker-management cooperation", began with expulsions of Communists and Left-Wing rank-and-filers from the Amalgamated Clothing Workers, from the United Mine Workers, and some other organizations. It was dramatized by the unseating and expulsion of the writer as a delegate to the Portland convention of the American Federation of Labor in 1923. More and more pressure was brought to bear on unions and Central Labor bodies for the expulsion of all members opposing the program of surrender to the employers. A special A. F. of L. "organizer" was sent into the Twin Cities to plan and conduct the anti-Red drive.

With visions of city, county and State offices before their eyes, with their reformist program endangered by the activity of Communists in the unions, the officialdom of the labor movement surrendered to the A. F. of L. executive council and began an expulsion campaign. The labor movement became moribund – sunk in the swamp of class collaboration.

The Trotzkyites deserted the revolution and have since then not only furnished ammunition to the trade union officialdom but took the lead in the struggle against the Party and revolutionary unionism. "Every deed has its own logic", and the defeatist tactics followed after the brilliant tactical achievements of the drivers' strike and the wide mass of sympathizers, resulting in surrender on the eve of victory, show that the Minneapolis labor movement has not yet fully recovered from the effects of years of class cooperation.

But *it is recovering.* And here it is well to state that without the work of the Communist Party, insufficient as it has been in some instances, *there would be no signs of recovery.* The influence of the Party can be seen in many ways already mentioned, but in no way more definitely than in the militant character of the strike movement and the obviously growing desire for and evidence of solidarity in struggle in the ranks of Minneapolis workers, organized and unorganized.

It is also obvious that the Minneapolis District of the Party has no easy task. The struggle to destroy the illusions about the Farmer-Labor Party cannot be conducted in the same way that a struggle is carried on against the Republican and Democratic Parties. They are supported by a skillful trade union bureaucracy, familiar with and able to use the stock terms of class struggle whenever necessary. It requires constant vigilance to understand and follow the maneuvers of these leaders; it needs patient and continuous exposure of them and warning of workers against them.

A reformist movement which produces a clever and unscrupulous Olson and a demagogue of the type of Congressman Shoemaker is not something that can be fought successfully only by jibes and ridicule and denunciation – although these too have their place. There is plenty of ammunition in the experiences of workers in the recent struggle. For example, although Shoemaker and his broomstick wand played a role on the picket line, it was Shoemaker who was telling the strikers of the danger of *federal* troops while Governor Olson was actually mobilizing the *National Guard* against the strike. Once the attention of workers is called to such things, they understand them without difficulty.

To work effectively, the Communist Party must have members in the unions. It must win the best union men for the Party. Its members must be active in the daily life and struggles of the unions. This is an indispensable condition for strengthening the labor movement against all its enemies – inside and out – for effective exposure and struggle against Farmer-Labor Party reformism and betrayal, for the political and organizational defeat of the Trotzkyites and their bureaucratic allies.

The rank and file of the Minnesota unions will support a revolutionary program now if the members of the Communist Party who present it are an integral part of the labor movement, bound to the working class with the unbreakable ties of its basic combat organizations – its trade and industrial unions.

If this condition is fulfilled, the Minneapolis working class and its organizations will rapidly gather and increase their forces, rally for a new and successful offensive against the employers' program of hunger and fascist suppression, will sweat out on the class battlefield the poison of Trotzkyism and Farmer-Laborism – and write a new and heartening chapter in the class struggle for themselves and the entire American working class. The Minnesota labor tradition, the recent militant strikes, the growing influence of the Communist Party, all point in this direction.

Part 2

Permanent Counter-Revolution

When the first Minneapolis truck drivers' strike came to a close last May, the Trotzkyites made high declarations about the "pre-eminent and unique" character of that strike. They claimed it was a strike "above the general run" with a "new method" and a "new leadership", etc.

The results of the second strike exploded the Trotzkyite boasts. The actions and deeds of the Trotzkyites during the second truck drivers' strike show them, not as the "leaven of principled Communists" as they hypocritically claim, but as a group of strikebreakers in the service of the bourgeoisie and its labor bureaucracy. Their duplicity and opportunism surpassed that of the most corrupt and degenerate labor bureaucrats. Every action and move of the Trotzkyites during this great strike bore out the statement of Comrade Stalin that "Trotzkyism is the vanguard of the counter-revolutionary bourgeoisie".

The two Minneapolis strikes have in a concentrated and very clear form exposed the Trotzkyite policies on the united front, on the question of social-fascism, on the question of revolution, as well as their reformist conception of strike strategy and tactics. To draw lessons and conclusions, we must note the outcome of the first strike, as well as examine the events and results of the second strike.

At the end of the truck drivers' strike in May, the Communist *Party* pointed out to the workers of Minneapolis that the settlement was a betrayal, that victory had been snatched out of their hands by the actions of their cowardly leadership. The first strike settlement made no provision for the thousands of workers who had joined the General Drivers Union during the strike and sent back to work without any gains the taxi drivers as well as others who had participated in sympathy strikes.

The Trotzkyites, on the other hand, boasted that the first strike was a great victory. If this was the case, why, then, was there a second strike? One of the issues involved was the question of who is-to represent the "inside" workers. But this was neither the chief nor the only cause foe the July strike. In the call for the second strike, issued by the General Drivers Local No. 574, we read the following:

> "The vital questions of wages and hours, which
> are of life and death concern to our members and their
> families, have been callously ignored. The right of the
> union to represent all its members – which was explic-
> itly agreed to in the strike settlement, have been de-
> nied. Seniority rules provided for in the agreement
> have been violated by the majority of the firms."

This statement by the union, itself, smashes the Trotzkyites' claim that the first-strike was a victory and proves that the analysis of the Communist Party was absolutely correct.

Trotzkyites Hang Onto the Blue Eagle

Both strikes have disclosed that the Trotzkyite attitude towards the N.R.A. is similar to that of the A. F. of L. bureaucracy. It is no accident that in both strikes, the most vital questions concerning the workers were left to arbitration and to the N.R.A. labor board. After the first strike, J. P. Cannon, writing in the *Militant,* claimed that the "Stalinists" were "slandering", the strike leadership – that the Minneapolis outcome was a "singular victory". He "admitted, however, certain "minor" mistakes. He wrote, for example:

> "Against these gains, must be put down on the other side the fact that the union agreed to submit the wage demands to arbitration and to accept the results."

We have already seen that these so-called "minor" errors led to the second strike. But let us read what Cannon has to say further on this. In the same article, we read:

> "This is a serious [Now it is no longer 'minor', but 'big' and 'serious' – M.C.] concession which the union officials felt necessary to make under the circumstances in order to secure the recognition of the union and consolidate it in the next period. It is a big concession that has been made by many unions."

Mr. Cannon's apologetic tone cannot cover up the essence of the question. It is the same excuse for class collaboration that Mr. Green might give, or any other labor faker, for that matter. It is true that such concessions have been "made by many unions", but the leadership of such unions, unlike the Trotzkyites, never made a pretense of being "Left revolutionists" who "fight compromise to the death", etc. The Trotzkyite viewpoint amounts to the recognition of the false conception that the workers secure their gains not through their own strength and class actions, but through collaboration with the employers and with the governmental agencies. Oh! says Mr. Cannon, we had to do this in order to get "recognition" of the union! Perhaps Mr. Cannon has heard of occasions when the government and employers do "recognize" unions, with an understanding, of course, that these unions are in the service of capitalism. There is also another form of recognition which results from the strength of the workers – as to this form, Cannon & Co. pretend ignorance. A few more such actions, Mr. Cannon, and President Roosevelt may consider your candidacy for the labor board and put you in proper strike-breaking company with the Greens, Lewises and the Hillmans.

When Cannon wrote the above-quoted statements, he still talked about the "next period". The "next' period" has come, and the union, under Trotzkyite leadership, *has once again surrendered the demands of the workers to the mercy of arbitration and the government.* Perhaps Mr. Cannon will once again tell the workers to wait for the "next period".

The draft thesis of the Trotzkyites states that:

> "It would be a mistake to fall a prey to the fraudulent ideas advanced by the Stalinists' Party that the new deal program is a fascist program. In the U.S. today, the potentialities of fascism exist primarily outside of the political state."

This is an ignorant and stupid defense of the class collaboration policies of the Trotzkyites, and exposes their servile attitude to the New Deal. In the face of the greatest terror unleashed against the working class of the U.S., the Trotzkyites spread illusions among the masses about the graciousness of the New Deal, thus disarming the working class in the face of the growing elements of fascism – yes, generating out of the State apparatus. For the Trotzkyites, compulsory arbitration, government mediators, raids on workers' headquarters exist primarily "outside the political State" – and General Johnson's fascist ravings are "unofficial". We wonder if "Marxists" like Cannon ever heard of a "non-political State"? (Shades of Lassalle and DeLeon.) We will refer these strike-breakers to Marx, Engels, Lenin, and Stalin.

It is *this thesis,* this line, that is put into daily practice by the Dunnes and Skoglunds, the Trotzkyite leaders of Local 574. In the *Organizer* of August 10, the official paper-of Local 574, we read:

> "Section 7-a of the National Industrial Recovery Act guarantees the right of independent labor organization."

If there is such an explicit "guarantee" in Section y-a, why then all the strikes and struggles for the right to organize – not only in Minneapolis, but everywhere in the U.S.?

At a mass meeting in Minneapolis, attended by thousands of workers, Miles Dunne, one of the Trotzkyite leaders of Local 574, made a declaration that "President Roosevelt abolished the antitrust laws for the benefit of labor, in order to permit combination of unions, to give a freer hand to industrial unions". This is a very original idea! Some other A. F. of L. bureaucrat could not gather the courage to make such an ingenious statement. Under the cover of "Left" phrases, the foulest traitorous deeds are carried out.

Betrayal – Not Victory

The second truck drivers' strike did not result in victory for the drivers, as the Trotzkyites claim. .The drivers carried on a heroic struggle, lasting five weeks; but in the end were compelled to go back to work with *no increase in wages and without union recognition. The most vital problems were once again lift to arbitration and the Labor Board.* Even the union is not secure because one clause in the settlement provides that a vote shall be taken among the drivers of 166 of the largest firms in Minneapolis to decide whether they want to be represented by Local 574 or by other representatives, which means the company union. The right of the workers to determine their own organization is surrendered in section 7 of the agreement which turns over the conduct of .the election to the employers and the regional labor board. The result of the election (the workers in more than half the firms rejected Local 574) confirms the statement of the Communist Party, District 9, that:

> "Such elections are used to drive out the workers' trade unions and to introduce company unionism with the direct help of the N.R.A. machinery. *This is not union recognition for which the strikers have been fighting.*"

Section 5 of the settlement specifically states that the inside workers shall return to work "but they shall not be eligible to vote in the election as called for in paragraph 7 hereof". This is a desertion of the inside workers. Recognition is allowed to them in only 22 firms. The young workers and temporary workers were also deserted by the statement in paragraph 8:

> "It is understood that the minimum wages herein specified do not apply to boys temporarily employed on small package delivery trucks, and they shall not be submitted to arbitration."

This hits the young workers employed by the biggest department stores. The question of rehiring is subject to a preferential list. This list is to be compiled by the employers. Already discrimination is taking place through the claim of the bosses that there is "no employment for all," at the present time.

It would be wrong to deny that the Minneapolis truck drivers, as well as the workers generally in that city, put up a militant struggle or that there were moments when the strike reached a high stage which could have developed into a general strike but for the leadership which set itself up as a wall to head off the militancy of the masses.

But the Minneapolis strike never reached the height of the San Francisco' strike. The difference was caused by the fact that in San Francisco there were leaders like Bridges, who struggled militantly against the labor bureaucracy and against the capitalists, while in Minneapolis, the Trotzkyites surrendered completely to the Farmer-Labor Party and the A. F. of L. bureaucracy.

Trotzkyites Hang Onto Coat-Tails of Olson

The Trotzkyites mock at the Communist conception of social-fascism. This position of the Trotzkyites naturally leads to their belief in the theory of the "lesser evil". This outlook is responsible for what took place in Minneapolis. If the theory that social-democracy develops into social-fascism is wrong, then it is justifiable to form a united front with Governor Olson and the Farmer-Labor Party, as well as the labor bureaucrats. This the Trotzkyites did. In both strikes they became an appendage to the politics and actions of the Farmer-Laborites and the bureaucrats of the Minneapolis Central Labor Union.

During the first strike, the Communist Party pointed out in official statements and in a series of articles by Bill Dunne, that if the strikers are to be victorious and win their demands, the role of Governor Olson must be exposed. But the Trotzkyites united with Olson. They resorted to the vilest distortions to cover up their alliance with Olson. They said that the Stalinists claim:

> "The essential object should have been the overthrow of the state government."

J. P. Cannon, writing in the July *New International,* argues that such ideas:

> "...have a logical meaning only to one who construed the situation as revolutionary and aimed at insurrection. We, of course, are for the revolution. But not today, in a single city."

It is very difficult to meet every silly argument of people who are artists at the game of distortion. The Communists never put forward the program of revolutionary insurrection during the Minneapolis strike. These nightmares originate in the heads of the Trotzkyites and in the capitalist press. The capitalist press went the Trotzkyites one better; they even predicted the day of the Communist uprising for August 16. It must have been very disappointing to the gutter press, as well as to the Trotzkyites that the uprising did not take place at 10:00 a.m. on the day "se". But it served its purpose. Governor Olson utilized this material, furnished by *agents provocateur,* as evidence before the Federal Court, in order to retain martial law in Minneapolis.

During the first strike, Governor Olson mobilized the National Guard, holding it in readiness in case of necessity. The working class of Minneapolis became suspicious of this action. But the labor fakers and the Trotzkyites assured the workers that they had nothing to fear from the "National Guard, that Governor Olson had mobilized the troops "for the protection of the workers". This deception was in part responsible, for allowing Olson to break the backbone of the second strike.

Despite the brutality of the Minneapolis police, the workers were on the offensive, and the mass picket lines succeeded in tying up all truck transportation. Only after Governor Olson had sent in the National Guard, did trucks begin to run as of normal, and picketing stopped. Governor Olson inaugurated a military permit system, so that before the strike was over, 15,000 trucks were running under protection of troops. The militia dispersed all picketing. Hundreds of the most militant strikers were thrown into the stockade. Did the Trotzkyite leadership mobilize the labor movement to fight for the most elementary rights of the workers? Absolutely not! When Governor Olson raided the union headquarters and the Central Labor Union offices, the rank and file was aroused and demanded action, there was a cry for spreading the strike, for a general strike. The Trotzkyites were compelled to react to the mood of the masses and give lip service to the general strike. But their lip service, too, did not last very long. The leaders of the Central Labor Union, Cramer, Weir and. Others, ordered the Trotzkyites to keep quiet about Governor Olson or they would have nothing to do with the strike. The labor fakers demonstrated their dissatisfaction with the Trotzkyites' "forgetfulness" by refusing to appear at a big mass rally at the Parade Grounds. The Trotzkyites were very quick in apologizing and in proving once again their loyalty to Olson

36

and the labor bureaucracy. In return for their promise, the labor fakers agreed to serve on the so-called union advisory committee.

Albert Goldman, a renegade from Communism, expelled by the Chicago District, acted as "labor" attorney for the truck drivers during the strike. He appeared before a mass meeting on August 6 and made the statement that he believed Governor Olson was not aware of the raid on the union headquarters. These words astonished the thousands of listeners who only a few days before had read statements issued by Governor Olson himself, justifying the raid on the union headquarters. The labor bureaucracy also justified the raid by claiming that Olson wanted to demonstrate that "the workers kept no store of arms, but were law abiding citizens". Olson's pre-arranged gesture in raiding the Citizens Alliance office allowed the fakers and the Trotzkyites to continue to spread lies about the "impartiality" of the governor. The Trotzkyites even went further than the A. F. of L. leaders. They openly stated that this was a move of Olson to the "Left" and that as long as he continued to move in this direction, they would support him 100 per cent. This statement was made by Goldman before 20,000 workers on August 6 – at the time when hundreds of rank-and-file pickets were being held in the stockade, sentenced to hard labor, and when picketing was completely prohibited.

The Trotzkyites and the union leadership of Local 574 did cooperate 100 per cent with Olson. During the last two weeks of the strike there was absolutely no picketing, by order of the union leadership. They instilled into the minds of the workers the belief that Olson would help them win the strike. Every time Olson executed a new maneuver with his military juggling, the Dunnes and Skoglunds created new illusions. It was not enough to tell the workers to depend on Governor Olson (the strikers were beginning to see things in their proper light). They, therefore, resorted to telling the workers that "it is impossible to picket in the face of the weapons of the militia". This is very familiar talk. We meet with it every time we run up against traitors who want to disarm the working class. Social-democracy uses similar arguments in order to prevent the working class from revolutionary action. We might remind the "new militants" that the workers of Toledo fought bravely even against the militia and we may add that the workers of Kohler, Wisconsin, continued their mass picketing in the face of militia. The workers in those places were probably fortunate in not having a "revolutionary leadership" of the Trotzkyite variety.

Trotzkyites for Martial Law

In the camp of the capitalist class, there was divergence of opinion about the best methods to use in breaking the strike. There was also the political situation in the State. The Republicans and a section of the employers' group did everything possible to embarrass Olson, to create the impression that he was not fighting hard enough against the strikers. The Citizens' Alliance (the organization of the employers) believed that it was possible to break the strike with the local police forces and appealed to the federal court for an injunction to lift martial law.

Because of this situation the Trotzkyites tried to create the impression that a blow at the Farmer-Labor Party and Olson is a blow at the workers. They linked the fate of the strikers with that of Olson. This conception covers up the fact that the chief class forces were the workers on one side and the bourgeoisie including Olson on the other. To place the problem differently would mean that the employers were more interested in fighting Olson than delivering a blow against the working class. This is a gross distortion of class relationships.

Every worker in Minneapolis knew that martial law was breaking the strike. What should have been the attitude of the strike leaders on this question? They should have fought most militantly for the lifting of martial law, not through the process of injunction, but by mass pressure and mass action. The motive of the bosses in trying to secure an injunction should have been explained, but the role of Olson should also have been exposed. The Trotzkyite leadership of Local 574 had a different view. At first they claimed in the *Organizer of* August 10:

> "We are not primarily concerned with this argument between the governor and the bosses. The bosses, of course, prefer the tactics of bloody Mike."

This means that martial law does not "concern" the union, although martial law was breaking the strike. Secondly, the union leadership indicated that they had a preference for bayonets of Olson's troops to that of bloody Mike (chief of police Johannes). More than that, the *Organizer* continues the defense of Olson and martial law in the following words:

> "A few hours after Olson, succumbing to the pressure of the aroused masses in Minneapolis and the whole State, interfered with scab trucking operations by the simple expedient of withdrawing military protection from them, the bosses hired themselves a bri-

gade of high-powered attorneys and applied for an injunction."

This statement contains a downright lie when it claims that Olson "withdrew military protection from the scab trucks". At the time that this statement was written, there were 11,000 trucks in operation – and a few days later, there were 15,000.

It takes the Trotzkyites, however, to put this question on a "higher plane". Albert Goldman once again gave advice to Olson. In the same speech where he defended Olson's raid on the union he told Olson that he should follow the footsteps of Debs (!!) who, "when an injunction was served upon him defied the injunction". What a mockery of history! Debs went to jail defying an injunction against the workers; Mr. Goldman urges his friend, Governor Olson, to retain martial law even though it breaks the strike!

The court sustained the rule of martial law. What was the reaction of the labor leaders to this? The *Minneapolis Journal* on August 11 stated:

> "Union leaders throughout the city expressed themselves without reservation as highly pleased with the decision."

Another labor leader, the head of the milk drivers' union, Pat Corcoran, a member of the union advisory committee, said:

> "The decision insures law and order in the city and prevents violence as the negotiators continue their deliberations."

The president of Local 574 is a man by the name of William Brown. He is a recently found "leader" of the Trotzkyites. He is the example of the "new militants", say the Cannons and Schachtmans. Let us listen to this new Trotzkyite recruit:

> "We are naturally pleased to see the governor's hand upheld in his declaration of martial law and I believe that the decision contributes to the development of conditions likely to end this strike."

This statement explodes even the fake paper opposition that the Trotzkyites offered to martial law. The fruit of the Trotzkyite policy, their collaboration with the Farmer-Laborites, is shown in the statement by another labor leader, Clifford Hall, who said:

"I am glad the strikers will not have to resume picketing."

This is the result of the Trotzkyite argument that the militia is in Minneapolis to help the strikers and that they therefore "do not have to resort to picketing".

To Cover Up the Strike-Breaking Role of the State

To cover up such crude strike-breaking, the Trotzkyites must find some theoretical defense. In such case, it is advisable to spout some phrases about "class relationships" in order to justify their attachment to Governor Olson. "Theoreticians" of the Trotzky camp, therefore, have come to the following conclusion:

> "The Farmer-Labor governor of Minnesota is pressed between two warring camps – between the workers and the capitalists, represented by Local 574 and by the Citizens' Alliance. Whoever exerts the greatest pressure will force this radical petty bourgeois to alter his course."

People must be either blind to believe this or, as in this case, must be willful traitors in order to spread the illusion among the workers that it is possible to utilize the bourgeois State apparatus for the benefit of the working class. Do the Trotzkyites mean to imply that what we, have in Minnesota is a "petty bourgeois State" – not a capitalist State? Here they are using the same arguments as the social-democrats who claim that fascism is a petty bourgeois movement, not a weapon of monopoly capital. They point to the social base of this movement and confuse it with its content. The Trotzkyites tried to do the same thing in relation to Minneapolis, That the Farmer-Labor Party receives its support from workers and farmers does not alter the fact that in essence the Farmer-Labor Party is a capitalist party; that, in modern society, the petty bourgeoisie does not play an independent role and the State apparatus is not a weapon of the petty bourgeoisie, but of the big capitalists to whom the petty bourgeoisie is attached. It makes little difference to the workers whether a petty bourgeois individual executes the orders of the capitalist class or a member of the big bourgeoisie.

The results of the strike-breaking acts of the State are the same. The Trotzkyites, however, to the very last moment, tried to save the face of Governor Olson as an "individual". Hugo Oehler, writing in the August 11 *Militant,* still sheds tears about "the most honest and sincere" man who "desires to help the working class". He would like to save Governor Olson from himself. He pities the poor petty bourgeois radical who, irrespective of his "good intentions", is compelled to do things he does not want to do. The Trotzkyites will not state that some "supernatural" forces urged Governor Olson to commit his strike-breaking actions. Perhaps there is a "Marxian" argument for this? Messrs Cannon and Schachtman, if, you lack "philosophical" terminology, ask Max Eastman or Sidney Hook – they will give you a hand.

All of this Trotzkyite strike-breaking activity has for its purpose the dependence of the workers, not upon their own forces and strength, but upon the good will of this or that bourgeois politician. This is class collaboration.

Red Scare

How does it happen that the Trotzkyites were able to assume leadership of the truck drivers' union and of the strike? If we were to believe Cannon, everything was "planned" and "organized". However, a closer examination of the problem reveals that the Trotzkyites were able to *share* the leadership because the labor bureaucrats of the A. F. of L. and by organizing the workers, not on the basis of struggle for their demands and against capitalism, but by appealing to the most backward ideology of the workers. The Trotzkyites did not hesitate to praise the New Deal, to wave the flag and to open each meeting with the singing of the Star Spangled Banner. In the *Militant* of August 25, we read:

> "In Frisco, the cry of Communist tore a deep hole in the strike front. In Minneapolis, it was a complete dud. The leaders faced the issue squarely. They did not rush into print denying their accusations. Nor did they shout their opinions to the wide world."

Yes, they "did not shout their opinions to the wide world". They did everything possible to organize an anti-Red hysteria. Groups of misled workers and henchmen of Dunne and Skoglund were organized to beat Communists, to tear Communist leaflets out of the hands of workers.

But they did everything possible to hide their identity. The greatest calamity that could have happened to them would have been for someone outside of the employers to accuse them of being Communists. In their paper, the *Organizer,* they tried to laugh the Communist issue away.

Here is a sample of the way the Trotzkyites dealt with the Red issue. In a leaflet issued by Locals 574 and 120 to the petroleum workers, we find the following statement:

> "Don't allow the Red Scare to keep you from coming to this meeting. If we were 'Reds' and 'Communists', why haven't we pulled the petroleum industry out on strike where a large part of our organization is? For the reason that the oil companies have seen fit to negotiate wages and conditions for you."

We must agree with the Trotzkyites that they are not Communists, for if Communists were at the head of Local 574, they would not send their own members to scab while a part of their membership was out on strike. J. W. Lawson, secretary of the Minnesota State Federation of Labor, delivered a speech over the radio, in which he told the employers that if they would point out any Communists in the A. F. of L. or in Local 574, these would be immediately expelled from the Union. Did the Trotzkyites raise any objection to this statement? On the contrary, they printed a praising summary of Lawson's speech in the *Organizer* and conveniently omitted this portion.

At the Minnesota State Federation of Labor Convention, held at International Falls on August 22, the Communist Party distributed a leaflet exposing the strike-breaking role of Olson. This leaflet aroused the fury of the labor bureaucracy. Mr. Lawson again issued a statement which was printed in the Minneapolis press. He foamed at the mouth and cried:

> "I want to put this organization on record as having no responsibility whatever for distribution of incendiary literature and I want to call on the leaders of the legitimate labor movement to drive this element out of the halls in which they hold their meetings."

No fascist could make a better statement than this lackey of Governor Olson who is disguised as a labor leader. Local 574 sent a delegation to this convention. What did they have to say about this proposal of Lawson? William Brown, president of Local 574 got up and seconded the motion of Lawson and then tried to pass the thing over by reducing it to an absurdity. He said:

> "If they [the Communists] knew that their names were even so much as mentioned here, they would

hold a rally of their whole 70 members in Minneapolis and hail a victory. Let us ignore them."

This is "facing the issue squarely", says the *Militant.*

Servile lackeys are never secure in their position. The more they cringe before their masters, the greater the danger of losing favor with their masters. The Trotzkyites played their role in the strike. They helped to protect Governor Olson. It seems, however, that the labor bureaucracy feels that they no longer need the Trotzkyites. They have therefore begun a campaign to give the Trotzkyites the boot.

William Green sent in a representative of the Executive Council of the A. F, of L., Paul Smith, to begin this "purging" process. The first thing Mr. Smith did was to separate the gasoline station employees from Local 574 and organize them into a separate local with a charter direct \from the Executive Council. The Trotzkyites have been shouting about the fact that they have built an industrial union in Minneapolis, that they take no orders from Green or Olson. But no one ever saw a more whipped bunch of traitors than the Trotzkyites when this act was committed. They allowed this to pass by without a word of protest.

At the Minnesota State Federation of Labor Convention, Wm. Shoenberg, one of the leaders, dropped a significant phrase. He said that the settlement of the general drivers' strike would be followed "by an aftermath within the organization". In other words, the ground is being prepared to oust the Dunnes and Skoglunds, whose services are no longer required. Let Mr. Cannon shout himself hoarse about the "liberal construction" of the A. F. of L. unions and its "compensated advantages", etc. The Trotzkyites by their anti-Communist activity sowed the wind and they are reaping a whirlwind. We might add here that the militant workers, too, have accounts to settle with them, but for different reasons than those of the A. F. of L. bureaucracy.

Strike Strategy and Tactics

The Trotzkyites wish to make the labor movement believe that the tactics and strategy pursued by them in the Minneapolis strikes deserve to be duplicated elsewhere. Cannon, in the July number of the *New International,* says:

> "Policy, method, leadership – these were the determining factors at Minneapolis which the aspiring workers everywhere ought to study and follow."

Those that aspire to defeat the working class surely will utilize the Trotzkyites' method as an example, but the revolutionary workers will reject their example. The Minneapolis strike did not reach the high phase that was reached by the Toledo, San Francisco, or Milwaukee strikes. In San Francisco, because of the militant Left wing, it was possible for a long period of time to fight off the reactionary A. F. of L. bureaucracy and the employers, and to realize the general strike. The strike was broken because of the direct treachery of the A. F. of L. bureaucracy. In Toledo, the A. F. of L. leaders had to maneuver for many days before they could betray the sentiment for general strike which was endorsed by nearly 90 locals. In Milwaukee, too, the Federated Trades Council was compelled to vote for a 48-hour general strike just before the carmen's strike was called off. In Minneapolis, however, the Trotzkyites, in alliance with the labor bureaucracy and Governor Olson, never allowed the sentiment for a general strike to develop to a point where it could be realized. First of all, they prevented their own members from joining the truck drivers' strike; secondly, even two weeks before the strike settlement, they sent the taxi drivers back to work without any gains. Only a weak attempt was made to pull the St. Paul drivers out on strike. The A. F. of L. bureaucrats, through parliamentary trickery, prevented the strike. The Trotzkyites, in this case too, gave up for fear of displeasing the fakers or going over their heads.

The Communist Party, District 9, saw that the strike was in danger of being broken, that the only thing that would save the strike would be a renewal of mass picketing and a spreading of the strike. The Party, put forward the following proposals to the union membership:

> "All members of 574 shall be called off the jobs they have been sent to, and *picketing on a mass scale must be renewed.*
>
> "Committees of from 20 to 50 drivers must be organized to visit all local unions, shops, factories, car barns, unemployed organizations and all workers' organizations to ask those workers to lay down tools and join us in the fight, which is the fight of the whole labor movement against the Citizens' Alliance.
>
> "In order to unite the whole labor movement behind the drivers let us call immediately a *united labor conference,* with representatives from all labor unions, shops, factories and all other working class organizations, unemployed and employed. This Conference

shall decide the question of a *general strike,* with the object to fight for the rights of the workers to join unions of their own choice for, the right to picket, for freedom of speech and assemblage, the release of our brothers in the stockade and for the lifting of all military regulations, which threaten to break the strike. *We can learn from the experience of San Francisco,* that under the leadership of militant workers, such as Bridges, this can be done. The success of such a movement is unquestionable if the Committee of 100 acts decisively, breaks all connections with the agents of Olson."

This statement correctly pointed out that under the leadership of Communists, and not fakers like the Dunne brothers, these steps would have would have been taken a long time ago, and the strike would have been won.

These proposals met with great response from the union membership – so much so that the Trotzkyite leadership was compelled to begin once again to give lip service to the general strike. They adopted a very weak resolution, appealing to the labor movement for a 24-hour general strike and also issued a very weak statement to the Minnesota State Federation of Labor, knowing well enough-that the labor bureaucracy, the friends of Olson, would not endorse such a move. Even during the last week of the strike, it was still possible to organize a movement for general strike, but this could have been accomplished only over the heads of the leaders of the Central Labor Union, which, of course, the Trotzkyites also would not dare to do. This is how they stated the problem:

"In view of the concerted attack on Local 574 by all the forces of capital, is labor ready to bring its own reserves into action? That is the question. The answer rests, *first, with the leaders* of organized labor in Minneapolis, and second, with the rank and file of the individual unions with whom the power of decision rests." *(Organizer,* August 18, 1934.)

Here again, the Trotzkyites showed their true colors. If the answer rests "first with the leaders", there never could be a general strike; the Trotzkyites knew this as well as anyone else. However, they purposely stated the question in this manner because they, too, were not interested in realizing a general strike as was proposed by the Communist Party.

There were many local unions that were interested in initiating such action. They were only waiting for a call from Local 574. In fact, rank-and-file A. F. of L. groups in some locals did propose such a motion. Naturally, this was very difficult because the membership of the locals would say, you ask us to join in a sympathetic and general strike, but the local most seriously involved refuses to initiate such action. More than that, we are asked to join in a sympathetic strike while their own membership is kept at work – scabbing upon their own brothers. This argument was hard to meet; only the most conscious of workers could answer satisfactorily why such action must be taken in spite of the leadership of 574. But the responsibility for such reaction was upon the shoulders of the Trotzkyite leadership.

We notice that the Trotzkyites spout phrases about "reserves". The Cannons and the Schachtmans, as well as the Dunne brothers, in this case, show complete ignorance of the most elementary principles of strike strategy and tactics. At the time they shouted about the necessity to call out "reserves", the strike was already in its fifth week, with the backbone broken. We may ask: was it not somewhat late to begin calling for reserves at such a time? Why did you refuse and stand in the way of calling out the reserves when it was possible to do so, when it was possible to realize even the general strike and bring victory, not only to the drivers of Local 574, but to the labor movement of Minneapolis? Because you Trotzkyites were not interested in mobilizing such action.

The Trotzkyites want to make the workers believe that they are the incarnation of "modern" strike strategy and tactics. We believe that any honest worker who has been a member of a trade union for a period of time could teach these "new militants" a thing or two about strike strategy and tactics. Every worker knows that when you bargain with a boss, you must be careful not to surrender your demands in the first discussion, that you have to stick by the demands, that a concession is given only in the last resort, when there is no other way out. What did the Trotzkyite leadership of Local 574 do? In the very beginning of the strike, they surrendered all the original demands, including the point on wages, and endorsed the Haas-Dunnigan proposals. The employers, naturally, took advantage of this situation. The Trotzkyites hung on the coat-tails of Haas, even when this priest, acting as a government mediator, had already himself repudiated his own proposals. The mediators too knew that the union leadership was weak-kneed. They therefore threw overboard the original Haas-Dunnigan proposals and proposed a new set of proposals which won the endorsement of the employers. These proposals, of course, were a little too crude; they demanded, that the strike cease, that all be taken back to work, *except* strikers who had participated in "violence" during the strike. This meant black-listing the most active workers. Had the Trotzkyites accepted this proposal, they would have been doomed and crushed by the rank and file. They, therefore, began to maneuver to modify this proposal, and the agreement which they finally accepted was only a modification of the original plan proposed by the Citizens' Alliance.

Cannon, in dealing with the problem of strike settlement, says:

> "There is little to go by in the way of previous experience to aid the modern militants in determining how and when to settle strikes. Their predecessors did not settle any."

The world began with the birth of Mr. Cannon; and there were no strikes "settled" until the Trotzkyites appeared upon the scene.

We shall not waste any time to convince these traitors that there were strikes before they became famous as strike-breakers, and that there were settlements before they "settled" Minneapolis.

Shortcomings and Tasks of the C.P.

In dealing with the role of the Communist Party during the strikes, we cannot help but state that the Party was trailing behind events. The Party did not prepare for the second strike. One gets the impression that the Party depended too much upon spontaneity, waiting for things to happen. Comrade Stalin points out that the theory of spontaneity is opportunism, that it is a denial of the role of the Party as the leader of the working class, that it means taking the line of least resistance.

During the first strike, the Party was able to link itself up with the strikers, to participate actively in picketing and even to lead in the battle of the Market, which has since become famous. However, even in the first strike, the Party worked chiefly from the outside. There was no organized Party fraction or rank-and-file opposition group within General Drivers Local 574. In the period between the first and second strikes, the chief tasks of the Party should have been the building up of a strong Communist fraction and rank-and-file group. But this was not done. Thus, the Party during the second strike again found itself as an outside force.

The slogans and demands put forward by the Party were generally correct and helped to mobilize the masses in support of the truck drivers; but the Party could have been much more effective if it had carried on work inside the local union. This gave the Trotzkyite leadership the opportunity to raise the cry of "outsiders". The Party was the only organization that came forward openly and clearly in exposing the role of Olson and the relation of the Trotzkyites to the Farmer-Labor Party. Yet we must state that there was a tendency to hesitate in exposing the Trotzkyite local leadership more sharply. The Minneapolis membership is a new membership. Its ideological background is still low; it can be said that this accounted for a certain slump in activity during the latter part of the strike. It was brought out in many units that many Party members did not understand the political differences between the Communists and the counter-revolutionary Trotzkyites. Because of this, there was a tolerant attitude on the part of even some Party members inside Local 574 towards the Trotzkyites. These comrades, instead of putting forward a clear Communist position, allowed themselves to be swept along by mass sentiment.

A serious strike situation demands more from the Party than during so-called normal times. However, the Party was not prepared for such a situation. Precisely when the functionaries and the lower Party organizations should have utilized the utmost initiative, they failed to respond. True, it was difficult to work in the face of martial law and in the face of the anti-Communist drive carried on by the Trotzkyites, but Communists must find ways and means of carrying through their tasks. There was even hesitation when it came to the distribution of leaflets, so that the District was compelled to utilize extraordinary measures in this respect. Technical matters were also badly neglected. The responsibility for such a situation rests squarely upon the shoulders of the leadership of District 9. There was too much of a tendency to surrender in the face of martial law. It was only towards the end of the strike that attempts were made to hold demonstrations with Communist slogans, despite the National Guard.

Another weakness disclosed in the strike was the failure to mobilize and involve the unemployed. It is true that the unemployed at the beginning of the second strike did come to offer their assistance and solidarity and were turned down by the Trotzkyite leadership. But the unemployed should have been involved despite the Trotzkyites. This was done in the first strike, and could have been repeated during the second strike.

Here, however, we must note that even in the first strike the participation of the unemployed was not utilized to infuse the strikers with the slogans of the Party. We may even place the question whether the unemployed, although mobilized by the Party, did not become a mere adjunct under A. F. of L. leadership, by giving up its identity on the picket line.

Conclusions to Be Drawn from the Strike

District 9, as well as the Party generally, must draw some conclusions from this last strike. The first and immediate task is the building of a Communist fraction among the truck drivers; then, by all means, a rank-and-file opposition group must be organized in Local 574. There is sentiment for such n movement after this latest betrayal. The workers are beginning to learn through their own experiences of the traitorous deeds of the Dunne brothers. Secondly, the Party apparatus must be educated and organized to act more decisively during extraordinary situations, both technically and ideologically.

Discussions should be organized in the units and classes set up to educate the membership in elementary principles of Marxism-Leninism. We must make our position on the Farmer-Labor Party clear. Governor Olson and the Farmer-Labor Party have lately increased their demagogy about establishing the "cooperative commonwealth". It is necessary that we expose this fraud. This can be done by placing in opposition to the fake "corporate commonwealth" our slogan of a real revolutionary workers' and farmers' government – the dictatorship of the proletariat. In the literature issued by our comrades during the strike, this was neglected. Even the statement issued by the District Committee analyzing the strike betrayal, while being generally correct, fails to bring out these political conclusions. This problem is important in every district; but in Minnesota, where the Farmer-Labor Party is in power, this is especially important.

The Minneapolis strike should further make us realize that when the Party as a conscious force is missing, even the best intentions and policies remain scraps of paper. Finally, District 9 must build its base in the Twin Cities, and must not lean too much on the agrarian outside sections. It is this failure to crystallize a base in the Twin Cities that is responsible for the failure of the Party membership to respond more decisively during the strike. This will be clear to us when we understand what Lenin taught us about the hegemony of the proletariat. If the Party would derive its strength from the proletariat in the Twin Cities, the District as a whole will be stronger and will be able to give leadership to the toiling farmers as well.

Published by Workers Library Publishers
New York City
October, 1934